LIGHT

By

Steffi Cavell-Clarke

©2017
Book Life
King's Lynn
Norfolk PE30 4LS

ISBN: 978-1-78637-104-1

Written by:
Steffi Cavell-Clarke

Edited by:
Grace Jones

Designed by:
Danielle Jones

A catalogue record for this book
is available from the British Library

PHOTO CREDITS

Abbreviations: l-left, r-right, b-bottom,
t-top, c-centre, m-middle.

Front cover – Jenn Huls. 2 – Sergey Novikov. 4 – Brian A Jackson. 5– Tom Wang. 6 – Andrey Arkusha. 7 – Anna Jurkovska. 8 – vvvita . 9l – ILYA GENKIN 9m – Moises Fernandez Acosta 9r – wenani 9rb Hard Ligth . 10 – Gelpi JM. 11 – mik ulyannikov. 12 – Boris Mrdja. 13 – Djem. 14 – Alexey Repka. 15 – enn Huls. 16 – Pablo77. 17 – Pavel Kriuchkov. 18 – SuriyaPhoto. 19 – Wingedbull. 20 – Soloviova Liudmyla. 21 – Galyna Andrushko. 22l – CPM PHOTO. 22r – StockPhotosArt. 23 – Johanna Altmann.
Images are courtesy of Shutterstock.com.
With thanks to Getty Images, Thinkstock Photo and iStockphoto.

CONTENTS

Words that look like this can be found in the glossary on page 24.

What is SCIENCE?

Where does light come from?

What helps us to see all of the colours in a rainbow?

Why can't we see in the dark?

Science can answer many difficult questions we may have and help us to understand the world around us.

What is
LIGHT?

Light is very important because it helps us to see all the things and people around us.

When there is no light, it is dark.
We can't see in the dark.

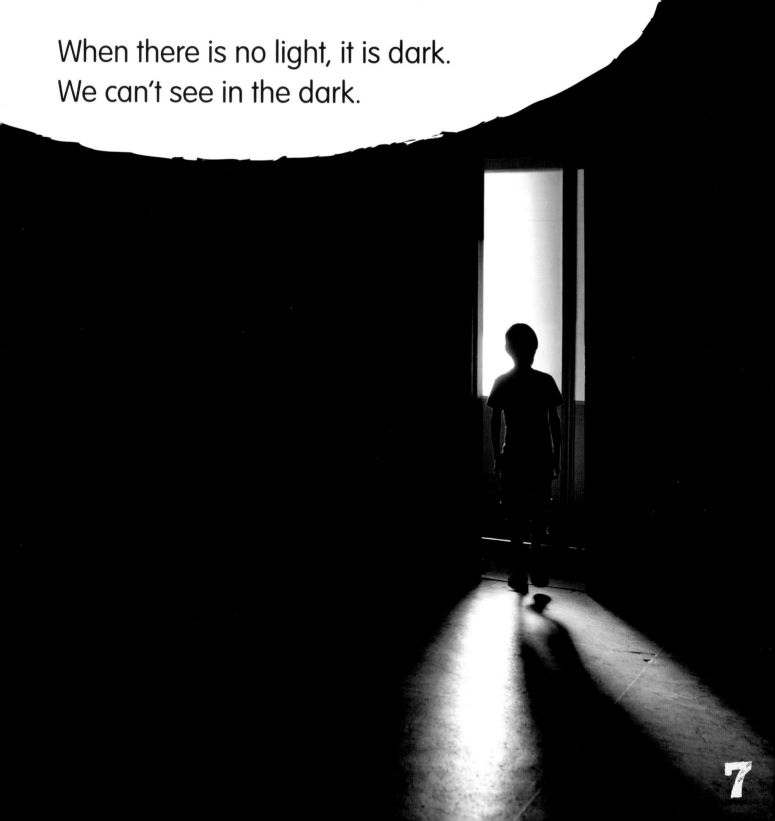

Where Does LIGHT Come From?

Light can come from many different places. These are called light **sources**.

Torches, lamps and lighthouses are all light sources. Our biggest light source is the sun.

Lighthouse

Torch

Sun

Lamp

9

How Does LIGHT MOVE?

Light moves from its source in **waves**.
The waves move in straight lines.

Light is always moving. The **speed** of light is very, very fast. It is the fastest moving thing on Earth.

We should never look directly at the sun because it might damage our eyes.

How Do We SEE?

Pupil

People and animals need light to see. Your eyes take in light through your **pupils**.

A special part of your eye, called the lens, makes a picture from the light and sends it to your brain.

Lens

What is SUNLIGHT?

The Sun is a **star** that gives planet Earth light and warmth. Every living thing on Earth needs sunlight.

Sunlight allows people and animals to see in the daytime. Plants also need sunlight to grow.

15

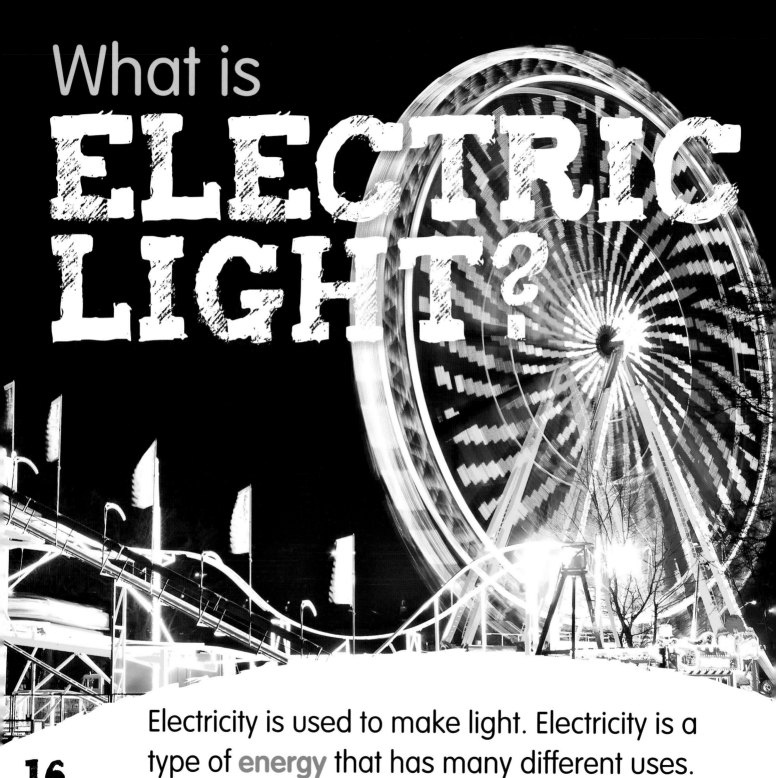

What is ELECTRIC LIGHT?

Electricity is used to make light. Electricity is a type of **energy** that has many different uses.

You can use electricity to switch on electric lights at home when it is dark.

What are COLOURS?

Green

Red

Blue

We can see many different colours.
What colours can you see around you?

Light is made up of different colours. When light waves travel through rain, it shows all the light's colours.

This is called a rainbow.

What are SHADOWS?

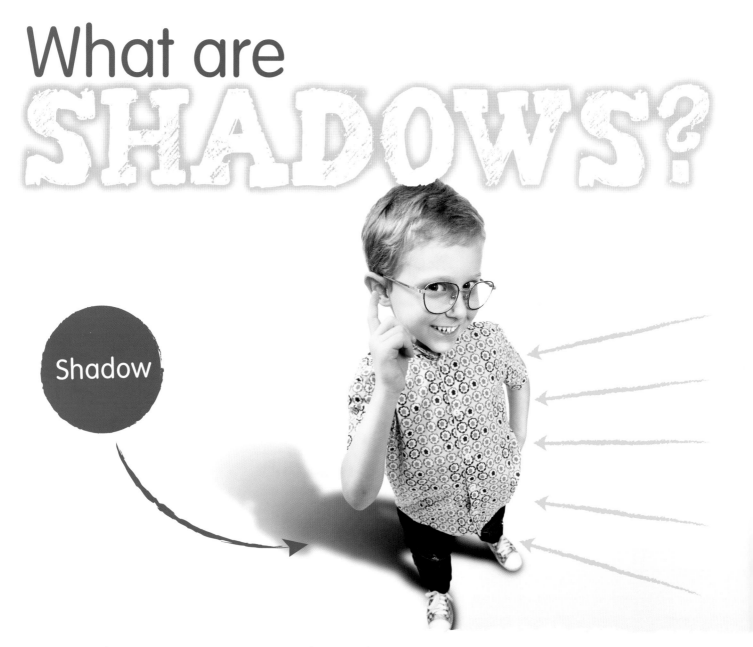

Shadow

Light waves cannot bend or go around corners. So when an object or a person blocks the light waves, a shadow is made.

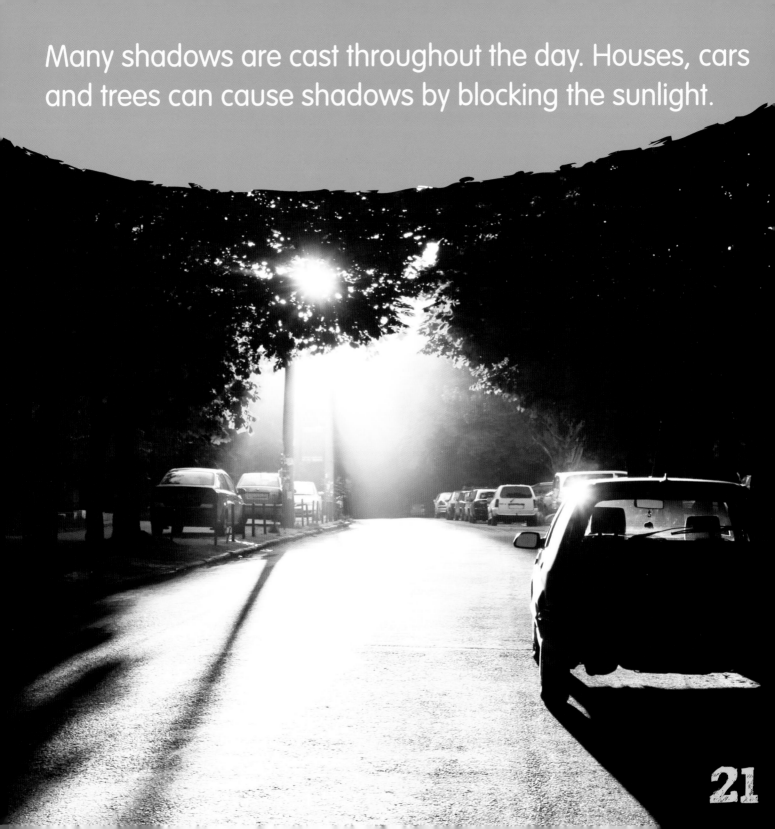

Many shadows are cast throughout the day. Houses, cars and trees can cause shadows by blocking the sunlight.

Let's EXPERIMENT!

Do you know how to make a shadow? Let's find out!

YOU WILL NEED:

Black paper
Scissors
Sticky tape
Straw
Bright Torch

STEP 1

Make a shadow puppet by asking an adult to cut out a shape from the paper. Attach the shape to the straw with sticky tape.

STEP 2

Switch the torch on and place it on a table facing a wall or sheet.

STEP 3

Hold the puppet in-between the torch and the wall.
Can you see the shadow it makes?

TOP TIP:
Ask an adult to help you!

RESULTS:

You should be able to see how light shines from
its source and casts a shadow when it is blocked.

GLOSSARY

energy	power used for an activity
pupils	special parts of the eye that let light in
sources	where something comes from
speed	how fast something moves
star	a giant ball of hot gas in space
waves	how something moves, usually in a back and forth motion

INDEX